Do It
Today

An
Encouragement
Journal

by Kara Cutruzzula
illustrated by Tyler Spangler

ABRAMS IMAGE, NEW YORK

Introduction

What does a meaningful life look like to you?

Perhaps it involves being present for your family, friends, colleagues, or community. Perhaps it's a life in which you unapologetically move toward milestones and dreams that feel authentic and worthwhile. Perhaps it starts with casting off old beliefs, embracing new growth, and experiencing a sense of momentum.

A life overflowing with meaning is possible. We're going to get there—together.

* * *

"I feel like I'm wasting my life."

I can't believe I said that out loud. But I did. Multiple times. Over multiple days. To multiple people. Where did that thought come from? I would like to blame the ongoing pandemic, or grief, or a work assignment, but the truth behind this dramatic statement was much simpler: I was spending very little time each day doing meaningful work.

Let's define *work,* because I'm not talking about the work that checks items off a to-do list. I'm talking about any work that requires effort and motivation, whether that springs from your career, art, personal life, or all the above. Rethinking what work looks like can shift your perspective. The good kind of work can be going outside for a long walk or putting in hours on a project that is important to you, like nurturing a side business, going back to school, or learning a new creative practice.

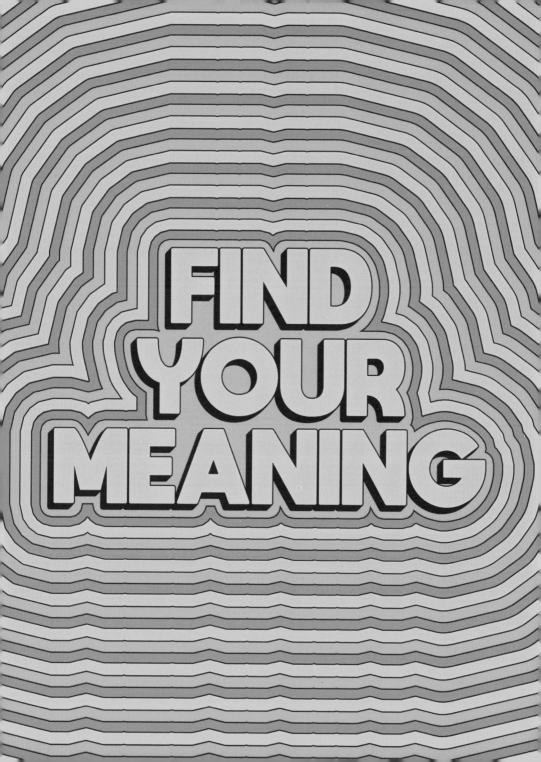

So what makes work *meaningful*? This work is the hardest and most essential there is, the kind you were born to do. Meaningful work makes your brain tired in all the best ways. When you're fully immersed, reaching the full range of your capabilities, all that time and energy feels worthwhile. It feels *right*.

That's what I wanted to find again: meaningful work; work that gave meaning to my days. I am a writer, for better or worse (writers love self-deprecation!), and I come alive when I write plays and musicals, poems and short stories. Taking a tiny idea from my brain, floating it into the world, and hoping it might reveal some truth to whoever finds it is meaningful to me. When I'm doing this work, I feel more confident, funnier, happier, lighter. I'm able to show up as a better partner, sister, daughter, friend, and collaborator.

So why is it extraordinarily difficult to find work that lights us up? And if we do find it, why do we resist giving it the time it deserves? Here's the truth: It's hard trying new things and changing our habits. Inertia is a powerful force, and it's disorienting to balance our current lives with dreams of what life could be. It's hard to be grateful for what we have while wanting something more. And it's hard to feel all these things at once.

Combine that with the urgent itch that you must figure everything out *right now,* on top of all your other responsibilities. Impossible! Finding the time to grow is almost as difficult as finding the work that makes you grow. Tomorrow always feels like the better, safer option, until tomorrow comes.

Maybe you feel like you're not in a space to begin—it's too late, you're out of options, or you're overwhelmed. Maybe you're tucked away in your burrow—that dark, quiet place where it's easy to hide from the future.

I feel those emotions, too. Sometimes they hit at the same time, and sometimes they're sprinkled throughout the week like existential confetti. I don't promise to have all the answers—I'm still figuring it out with you. But I hope to share the lessons and observations I've returned to again and again. When I remember and use them, I get closer to the person I see in the mirror on my best days.

Lately, it might feel like nothing has gone as planned. We have changed, mourned, struggled, and survived. Together, we have learned that tomorrow holds no promises. If ever there was a time to do something new, why not now?

There is no better moment to reinvent yourself or discover new possibilities. There is no doubt you've changed in the past few years—perhaps in the past few days—and are getting serious about what the next version of your life looks like. You've also probably had some ideas about what you'd be happy to leave behind.

Look around. The people beside you are switching careers, embracing hobbies, and starting new adventures. While it may appear like everyone is uprooting their lives, they're actually growing new roots. They're digging deeper, and you can, too.

THERE IS NO BETTER TIME THAN NOW

This journal is an unlimited space for your best days. You are someone who makes things (or wants to). Someone who has dreams (or wants to define them). Someone who is searching for motivation (or wants to shake up their routines).

You want to feel like you're spending time on the commitments, ideas, and people that give your days meaning. You care, deeply, about the work you do and what you are giving back to the world. You long to move toward the future with bright ambition and a sense of beginning.

You will follow your curiosity.

You will start before you're ready.

You will percolate your ideas.

You will find courage to fly.

You will show off your rejections with pride.

You will connect with your champions.

You will share your generous spirit.

You will cultivate optimism.

Look ahead. The space before you contains the blueprint you will create, the call to action that comes from your voice, and the gentle push that begins your most meaningful life.

Do it today.

CHAPTER 01

Go Toward
Your Nerves

Why was there a notebook on my coffee table with the word LYRICS written across the cover in black marker?

I recognized my scraggly handwriting, but I didn't read music or play an instrument. I did take piano lessons when I was a kid, but quit when my instructor wanted to stick to basic theory and refused to teach me how to perform "Part of Your World" from *The Little Mermaid*. But now, I was thirty years old and I'd never written a song. I had no idea how to write a song.

Still, something compelled me to try. Even the idea of trying was exhilarating, and I had decided that this notebook would hold all the songs swimming inside me—a physical manifestation of my unhatched skills. Over the months that followed, my attention was drawn back to those pages, and I'd write a line or two, try to rhyme some words that definitely did *not* rhyme, and scribble phrases that might prove useful in some mysterious future version of my life.

I didn't realize it at the time, but I was experiencing the magic of the pull. An invisible magnetic pull happens before starting something new. When you're quiet and still, you feel the tug. *Look over here*, it says. *Aren't you intrigued?*

That's what the notebook told me: *Follow the pull*, despite that my past experience did not align with this action; the

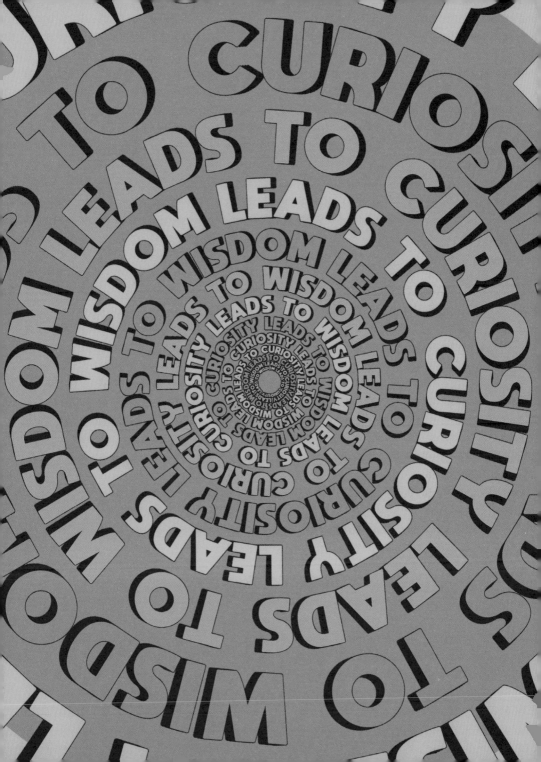

hurdles were high (I had no clue what I was doing); and nothing about it made sense.

Picking up that notebook made me *nervous*. What if I failed? What if my friends laughed at me? What if I wasted my time?

I would love to tell you that the first song I put to paper became a *Billboard* No. 1 hit, but that didn't happen. Instead, life took other unexpected directions, and I gained something even more valuable. I saw the power of following the pull.

Signs of the pull are often a sense of excitement, or simple curiosity. That's what my notebook gave me, and I recognized the same feeling a year later when I saw an announcement about a lyric-writing class. The class was at capacity, but I couldn't stop thinking about it—there was the pull—until I finally asked if there was a waiting list. There was. I got in. And on the first day of class, sitting in that room full of strangers, learning about song form and rhyme schemes, I understood why I created that lyrics notebook. This was where I was meant to be.

I left that class with a few songs—nothing set to music, but enough to apply to a prestigious musical theater workshop. I was invited to audition, which involved reciting my lyrics out loud to seven intimidating composers and lyricists sitting behind a very long table. I was nervous again, yet I felt the insistent pull to try anyway. I got in. After four years in the workshop, I've bonded with new friends, collaborated on writing musicals, and am fully immersed in a new world.

I never could have guessed all this would happen from a notebook.

What's so exciting about being pulled forward is the chance to head down a new path.

Now, for every pull, you will probably experience its opposite: *the push*. Other experiences can repel us, often because they feel like a step backward, or a lateral move, or no longer offer growth. The spark is gone.

Have you ever been overwhelmed by this feeling? Perhaps you were reading a job posting, eyes dancing down the list of responsibilities, and your brain said, *Run!* That's an obvious sign of being pushed away. Sometimes the opportunity might look impressive on paper—it's hard to resist an ego boost—but the work itself sounds exhausting or soul-crushing. You think, *Something about this doesn't feel right.* That's an important feeling, too. And when you close the browser tab, say no to the offer, or turn in the opposite direction, a familiar comfort takes over: sweet relief.

You're relieved because you don't want to go that way.

You're being pushed away for a reason. Reflect on why you're being repelled. What makes that direction feel so uncomfortable? Maybe the opportunity would have made sense a few years ago, or it's simply not drawing you in. The push is a valuable signal telling you not to go backward.

Compare that to the attraction of the pull. Maybe you don't have the "right" skills, feel out of your depth, or can't explain why you're drawn to this new space, but there's that invisible thread again. Curiosity. The pull leads you to possibility—even if it arrives with nerves, fear, and maybe confusion.

Where is the pull leading in your own life?

Maybe you're surprised to find yourself immersed in a new hobby, intrigued by a different career, or you're considering taking a class out of your comfort zone.

You might not know exactly where you're going, but have faith: A new path awaits. This is where you're meant to go. And now you're going to find the courage to follow the pull.

FOLLOW THE MAGIC OF THE PULL FORWARD

What is pulling you forward?

What is pushing you away?

_____

_____

_____

_____

_____

_____

_____

_____

_____

_____

_____

_____

WHAT IS PUSHING YOU AWAY NO LONGER SERVES YOU

Think about a major turning point in your life.

Maybe a graduation, a move, a breakup, or a new job. Remember what it felt like right before the big change.

Were you scared? How did you move ahead anyway?

_____

_____

_____

_____

_____

_____

_____

_____

_____

_____

_____

Being nervous
churns your
stomach, but it's
also a signal that
you care about the
outcome.

**What is making you a little
nervous right now?**

Are you afraid of failure?

What's the worst thing that could happen?

Pretend you're standing in front of seven people about to judge your work.

Good news! They love it.

Write down every positive comment they share with you.

- _____

- _____

- _____

- _____

- _____

- _____

- _____

Consider the last message you received that made you excited.

What was it about? Who was it from?

What direction is it pulling you in?

Routines can help
us organize our
days.

**What is one new routine
that would benefit your life?**

When would you like it to
begin?

Routine:

_____

_____

_____

_____

_____

Start Date:

_____

CHAPTER 02

Start Before You're Ready

We are never ready for the events that shape our lives.

When you left home for the first time, or started a family, or asked your boss, "Do you have a minute," right before quitting, you might have been excited about the change, weighed all your options, created a plan, and finally jumped.

But look back at these moments. If you're honest with yourself, were you 100 percent ready? Did you know *exactly* what was going to happen next?

Everyone has fears. Even the most prepared, talented, and accomplished people are sometimes scared to begin. (In fact, sometimes they're the most scared.)

Fear helps us delay big decisions until those decisions are made for us. Fear leads to choosing our college major at the last possible moment, or tolerating a job we're not crazy about for "just a little while longer." Fear is very good at keeping us cozy—until outside forces barrel in and tell us it's time to move on, whether we're ready or not.

Outside forces can grant us accidental gifts, even when they shake up our lives. We learn to start again, because there is no other choice. We walk through the world knowing that things we once considered constant can also be lost. And as we find ourselves emerging from these moments of uncertainty, grief, or pain, something

YOU NEVER KNOW UNTIL YOU DO IT

incredible happens. Our sense of what we thought possible expands. We find courage we didn't know we had.

Outside forces show us how strong we can be.

The lesson is to apply these experiences to the act of beginning—over and over again.

For all your major moments and milestones, you must start before you're ready. In fact, you can start before you're ready when it comes to the smaller tasks, too. You might be reluctant to make an overdue doctor's appointment or ask a favor of a colleague. Cue the excuses: there will be a better time, or you still need more information. Maybe that's true, but none of us will ever be eager to get uncomfortable or scared, in the same way we may hesitate before starting a new project or applying to a dream opportunity. Comfort feels safe, so we sink into it. The days pass, our lives pass, and we wake up one morning and wonder, *Why didn't I ever do the things I wanted to do?*

You will never feel completely ready for the projects that scare you, for the levels of creativity you think you need in order to do your best work. You may not believe you have the courage to change locations or careers. You will hedge and debate. (If you're like me, you might overanalyze for years.) You drag the important tasks from one day to the next on your calendar, telling yourself in a kind and understanding tone, *I'll just do it tomorrow.*

The illusion of tomorrow is beautiful, perfect, and completely spotless. Tomorrow is all promise. Because we want the best for ourselves and our projects, our seeds of creativity and business ideas, our dreams and pristine drafts, we believe that waiting until tomorrow is the correct choice.

But it's not.

Tomorrow will fail you. Not in any grand or catastrophic way, but through an inevitable winnowing of hours. Your meeting will run long, your car might break down, you get sucked into a TikTok scroll. Every free minute will attach itself to a task. You arrive in the evening looking for the thief who made off with your day and, by extension, with your life. *Where did the time go? Wasn't tomorrow supposed to be different?*

Many of us have spent years promising ourselves to start *something* tomorrow. But we need to admit that *tomorrow* isn't the solution.

Today is the day to begin. You may not finish every task or fulfill every goal, but you can make a commitment to yourself—to your projects, dreams, and future—that you refuse to wait any longer. You can look back on your history of pushing through uncomfortable moments and moving forward without every answer and trust that those experiences have prepared you for this one. Always have faith you are better off leaping rather than standing still.

We are not starting today because we're ready, but because we know we will *never* be ready. Admitting that no absolutely perfect moment exists means that every moment is full of promise.

Life doesn't wait until we are ready. Life happens anyway. Isn't it time to begin?

HAPPINESS BELONGS IN YOUR HANDS

What does being ready feel like?

TOMORROW IS
AN ILLUSION
TOMORROW IS
AN ILLUSION
TOMORROW
AN ILLUSION

Time to get
everything out
of your head and
onto the page.

**Create a rough draft of the
next step of your project.**

You don't have to be a writer
to write this down. Get it out
anyway.

_____

_____

_____

_____

_____

_____

_____

_____

_____

_____

Is there one conversation you're not ready to have?

Even if you don't know what to say, or how to say it, begin here by writing a few possible opening sentences.

Consider the finish line for your project.

Now imagine the finish line is moved up to—oh boy!—the end of today.

What would you do right away?

Forget nouns. Be a verb instead.

List every word that describes the forward motion you want to feel right now.

- _____
- _____
- _____
- _____
- _____
- _____
- _____
- _____
- _____

YOU ARE SPRINTING, SOARING,

STARTING

What action would you take today if you felt fearless?

_____

_____

_____

_____

_____

_____

_____

_____

_____

_____

_____

_____

_____

What's one thing you plan to do tomorrow that you could actually start today?

Sometimes seeing all you've accomplished in one place is the best type of encouragement.

What did you start this week? Even the smallest steps count.

What will you continue?

Have you been debating making a big decision?

Get out all your current thoughts and feelings on that choice right here.

_____

_____

_____

_____

_____

_____

_____

_____

_____

_____

_____

_____

_____

_____

_____

_____

CHAPTER 03

Don't Be Productive, Percolate Instead

John Steinbeck needed a warm-up. Every day, before attempting to hit his self-prescribed goal of one thousand words, the novelist would sit down and write something entirely removed from the sights and sounds of Salinas Valley. He would dash off a letter to his editor.

The letters served as a kind of free-flowing daily diary, chronicling his creative process, struggles, personal life, and dwindling pencil supply. They also served as a highly achievable goal for the future Nobel Prize winner. First, complete an easy task: a message to a friend, where he could empty his mind of doubts and fears. Then, only after he ran out of things to share, would he return to writing *East of Eden*.

We are a culture obsessed with productivity. I know this too well, as I've written thousands of words and dozens of articles about how to improve your time-management skills, juggle competing priorities, and force creativity to sprout in even the driest soil.

But now, I'm slightly relieved to report, old-fashioned productivity is dead. This may sound wild coming from a recovering productivity pusher, but there is a growing realization among folks across industries and disciplines that perhaps we've been going about this all wrong. We make lists, download apps, and create systems to maximize . . . what, exactly? Time? Output? Money? The hustle and grind might fill your calendar, but it won't fill your soul.

EVERY
LITTLE
BIT
OF
GOOD
ADDS
UP

So how do we balance our overwhelming desire to achieve our goals and avoid flaming out? The answer isn't producing more, but rather embracing our ability to percolate.

What is percolation, exactly? Percolating means giving yourself time and space to think *without* the extra pressure to track your performance. It's allowing yourself to enjoy reflecting and exploring your options. You don't have to come up with a fully formed, ready-to-deploy idea. You're just coming up with *stuff*. The whole process is also a lot more fun.

Percolation comes with understanding you have access to an endless stream of ideas, avenues, and solutions. It's knowing that these possibilities are constantly brewing, even on your less "productive" days. It's believing in the long game and knowing you're heading in the right direction.

Steinbeck understood that process. He used the letters to percolate his thoughts and trusted that the right words would arrive when he needed them. Even when he was fretting about writing, he was committing himself to writing.

Unlike traditional productivity practices, percolating doesn't have a finish line. We must remember that even if we don't hit our word count or win that prize, it's going to be OK. We must have faith that there is always more inside of us: more creativity, more curiosity, more connection, and more chances to try again.

Percolation happens when you have a lightbulb moment during your commute or meet a friend of a friend who has the answer to a question you didn't know you were asking. Our minds are always working toward solutions and puzzling out options, whether we're conscious of it or not. Percolation is organic—and it's happening all the time.

Compare that to productivity tricks, which promise to (and sometimes do) corral our brains.

Don't get me wrong: I love tricks, tips, and hacks. Over the years, I've been an advocate of the Pomodoro Technique, which involves working on one task for twenty-five minutes, taking a five-minute break, resetting the timer, and starting again. I've also shut off my Wi-Fi, embraced airplane mode, worked on group Zooms, created color-coded schedules and digital workflows, batched my email, sectioned my days into "maker" and "manager" silos, and tried dozens of other methods to work faster, smarter, or harder. They all help—to a certain extent . . . and usually for just a little while.

There's a reason they stop working. Productivity is measured in strict intervals. How much did I get done before lunch? Today? This week? You are forced to constantly generate that start-up energy and measure your progress. And anytime you're not *producing* can feel like time wasted.

Percolation embraces the opposite of this constant hustle. Living and working should not be enemies fighting for your time and attention. A walk in the park can give you rest or enjoyment if you are not multitasking by knocking out that new podcast episode or jumping on a conference call. Dinner with your family or friends can be a pleasure when you are not checking your phone every five minutes. Trust that slowing down isn't going to stop your momentum— instead, it will save you. Your ambition, energy, and goals don't need to be deliberately and consciously fed 24/7, because subconsciously, you are always percolating. This is why problems feel lighter after a good night's sleep. Have faith that you are making strides all the time, regardless of when the timer is beeping.

When you do feel ready to act, sit quietly and ask yourself, *What is the one thing I know I need to do next?*

In those moments, all that unseen percolating adds up. You might not like what you need to do next. Maybe it's a boring administrative chore (taxes!), a thorny creative task, or difficult conversation with a colleague. But you'll always have a response, because you've been working toward an answer the entire time.

Percolating also allows for creative cross-pollination. You might read an article and get an idea for a side project. Or you overhear a conversation with a bit of dialogue you want to steal. Or you read a story about an octogenarian going back to school that inspires you. Everything that crosses your path is adding up to help you decide your next move.

How many times have you described a problem to someone and, at the end of your monologue, realized the solution was right in front of you? That's because you— yes, *you*—are the deepest wellspring of advice. Not your to-do list. Not the wisdom you find in a wonderful keynote speech. Your ability to keep going surpasses any system or hack you might drop after a week. You know your own history and what worked for you in the past. There is no one-size-fits-all solution, so take the pressure off when the productivity hack *du jour* doesn't revolutionize your life.

You don't need more advice about what to do. You need the courage to face what you know you must do.

Let yourself percolate and consider possibilities. Write a letter. Listen to music. Call a friend. Look inside and untangle what feels impossible to understand in your brain. The answers are already within you.

Together, we're going to find your next step and discover sparks to keep you going.

HUSTLE AND GRIND MIGH
FILL YOUR CALENDAR,

BUT WON'T
FILL YOUR SOUL

List five systems,
tricks, or hacks
you've used in the
past.

How did they help you?

How long did they last?

1. _____

_____

2. _____

_____

3. _____

_____

4. _____

_____

5. _____

_____

Often, we tell ourselves we need unlimited free time to work on a project.

But those uninterrupted hours can speed past, and we might not accomplish as much as we thought.

Let's get honest. How much time do you actually need to take a small step today?

YOU ARE MORE POWERFUL THAN YOUR PRODUCTIVITY

If someone were to ask,
"How are you today?"
what is your honest answer?

Environment affects our moods, processes, and (yes!) ability to percolate.

Where is a motivating place for you to work? Explain why and how it inspires you.

_____

_____

_____

_____

_____

_____

_____

_____

_____

_____

_____

_____

_____

_____

Taking your brain in a different direction can help clarify your thoughts.

Write down ten ideas completely unrelated to your current project.

Some examples: ten countries you'd like to visit, ten song or book titles, ten items from your childhood bedroom.

1. _____

2. _____

3. _____

4. _____

5. _____

6. _____

7. _____

8. _____

9. _____

10. _____

Picture a younger version of yourself—age eight, fifteen, thirty-four, fifty-seven, you name it.

What would that person say about where you are now?

FIND YOUR ENERGY

You can still protect your time and energy while you percolate.

What is one habit or method you use to recharge yourself? Describe it in detail here.

What is your biggest dream?

What's the first thing you can do to work toward achieving it?

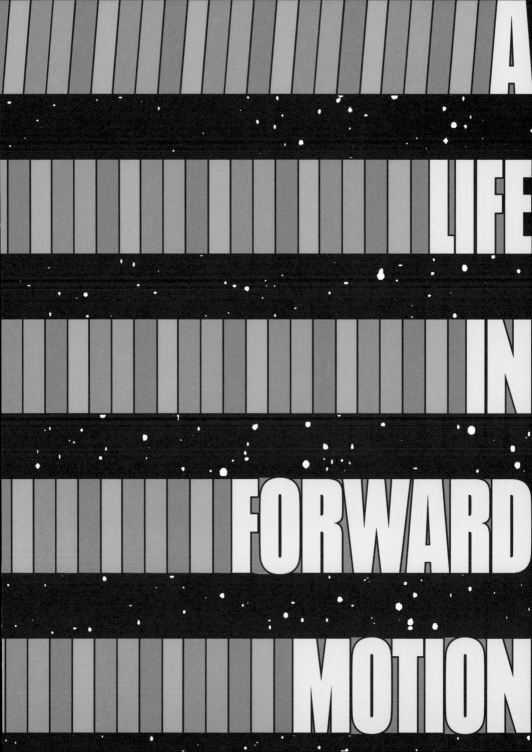

A
LIFE
IN
FORWARD
MOTION

CHAPTER 04

Stamina, Courage, and Mirages

A black-and-white warbler is a beautiful bird.

Tiny, the size of a petite person's palm, with zebra stripes running the length of its body, this little creature migrates twice a year from as far north as Canada down to South America or back, flying thousands of miles in search of warmer weather. But during its journey, the warbler can encounter predators, nasty storms, and another disastrous obstacle: the towering buildings of the Manhattan skyline.

From the sky, warblers look down and see an enormous patch of green known to us as Central Park. Here's a perfect pit stop. Fresh water, delicious bugs—what could be better? The park is one of the great birding spots in the world, with more than 210 species visiting yearly.

But the shiny glare of surrounding buildings is confusing. The glass reflects trees and foliage, causing warblers to fly straight into the glass, thinking it's the refuge of the park. Their long expedition is cut short by a man-made mirage.

What do sweet birds have to do with your own expansive goals and dreams? Our doubts and fears are like those buildings. They are mirages, reflecting what we *think* we know, but would see are fake with a little investigation.

Birds follow a biological instinct to fly. Even though the distance is far and there are challenges along the way, they are searching for something and keep beating their wings to find it.

You are searching, too. Some days you manage to move forward even though you're exhausted. Some days you find that elusive flow state where you fully experience the joy of creating, making, and thriving. Some days you trust you are percolating and following the correct path.

Other days there seem to be obstacles everywhere. There is never enough time, money, or energy. You might see a glimmer of your ultimate destination, but it is hard to keep flying. You have the right to be tired. You do so much.

And yet. The quiet part of you—that deep, unquestioning instinct—knows you want to continue.

It's not your fault the mirage is distracting. Almost everything we encounter is designed to divert our attention. Just this morning, I've been thrown off course by sixteen emails, three text messages, the urgent need to buy more garbage bags, the sound of construction workers outside my window, and the fact that, allegedly, I need to update sixty-seven apps on my phone. I didn't even know I had sixty-seven apps.

Beyond the everyday diversions, our doubts and fears can also stop us in our tracks. Fear of failure or of not finishing. Fear of disappointing others or ourselves. Fear that we're not ready or we're too late. These doubts can suddenly shift or appear without warning.

How do we keep flying in the face of so much noise? Where do we find the stamina? Will we ever reach some impossible destination?

The trick is remembering to tune in before burning out. *Tuning in* means finding excitement, joy, or solace in our daily flights. It means focusing less on the endings and appreciating where we are in our journey. It also means accepting that each daily flight isn't a grind to overcome, a hustle to conquer, or a period to push through, but can instead hold meaning in itself. The fact that we can fly, today, is the reward.

The best way to find strength during low moments is to value every tiny beat of your wings, because each beat is a sign of progress.

There is no shame in burning out, either—sometimes I feel like I'm still recovering from a job I left back in 2012!—but there is always a way through. It takes time and effort to reset your body, brain, and beliefs after committing to something. Each experience is one data point and is not representative of every future company, project, career, or relationship. Soon, you will gather other experiences, unlearn some of what you believed to be true, and keep flying forward.

There is also no blame in burning out. Rewrite the story that it was all your fault. Take the time you need to recover, but when you're ready, know you must tune back in. Ask yourself what you want next. The answer might make you nervous or might convince you to remain still. That's OK, too.

But without courage or growth, we are choosing to live an older version of our lives.

Stay awake to choices.

I love when a friend calls and announces they're quitting their job. (For some reason, people love sharing this news with me. Probably because I love hearing about it so much.) Yet usually, moments after they tell me about the new offer, company, position, and salary bump, they say, "Well, maybe I could stay . . ." The possibilities seem endless—and some are more comfortable than others. Embracing the known over the unknown is easy. Familiar. Tempting. *What to choose?*

It's thrilling to have choices. Having options is a privilege. But there's one question we sometimes forget to ask. What if every decision in our lives was made based on the question: *Will this choice help me to grow?* You will never resent a choice that allows you to grow, but you might resent staying the same.

Now let's figure out how to look beyond the mirage, find courage, and keep flying.

TUNE IN, DON'T BURN OUT

What do you see
when you tune in
and ask yourself,
"What's next"?

What are some of the traits you admire most in yourself?

Think back to the
last time you felt a
sense of burnout.

What caused this feeling?

Have you ever had to ask someone to write you a letter of recommendation?

What if you wrote one for yourself, highlighting your strengths and what you would bring to your next opportunity?

Start it right here.

I am recommending myself for _____

_____

_____

_____

_____

_____

_____

_____

_____

_____

_____

_____

_____

_____

The word *deadline* can often inspire dread.

Instead, think of approaching deadlines as *milestones*.

What is one upcoming milestone that excites you?

PAST
ISN'T
PRESENT

Do you have any habits or behaviors you'd (gently) like to unlearn?

List them here and why you'd like to let them go.

X
_____

X
_____

X
_____

X
_____

X
_____

X
_____

X
_____

X
_____

X
_____

X
_____

Who is the most
persistent and
positive person you
know?

**What advice would they
give you about a challenge
you're facing?**

While migrating, a warbler travels thousands of miles.

How far have you traveled on your journey?

How many miles are there to go?

CHAPTER 05

Sweet, Sweet Rejection

Fail faster.

Embrace failure.

Sometimes you win, sometimes you learn.

Failure mantras are easy to say and even easier to dole out. But when we apply them to our own experiences, they can feel impossible to believe.

Every one of us can write a failure list describing what *hasn't* happened in our lives. (My own list includes being rejected from film school and playwriting programs, being turned down for screenwriting labs, film festivals, workshops, residencies, and plenty of jobs—the tally is endless!)

It's amazing how talented we are at replaying the lowlight reel, dreaming about our many unlived lives, rather than embracing the one life we're lucky enough to live.

Of course, when we're nudged to think about what *has* happened, a different list emerges, full of surprising wins, improbable paths, and unpredictable successes. Remember that your highlight reel is long, too.

Yet, we can benefit from viewing our failures, rejections, and missed chances as opportunities for new wisdom and growth, because they remind us what we truly care about.

THANK YOUR FAILURES

I recently talked to a friend who was up for a big job at a high-profile company. She had four interviews scheduled over two days, and the HR manager provided a list of twenty scenarios she might be asked to discuss. This friend spent hours prepping for the interviews (on top of working her current job and caring for a newborn). "I haven't used my brain this much in years," she told me. "And it feels *good.*"

That's because the things she did to stretch herself—putting in the hours, saying no to distractions, learning new skills, and taking a hopeful risk—were brave acts.

Dropping yourself in front of the tornado of possible failure requires a miraculous blend of faith and endurance. You must declare, *This is what I want, and this is what it looks like to go for it.*

I won't say that failing feels wonderful. Rejection can sting. If you feel awful for only ten minutes or so, that's essential information. The opportunity might not be as important as you thought. But if you stew about a rejection for six weeks—or even six months? Knowing you really wanted something is incredibly helpful. Here's why: Failure can be an anchor, advisor, and motivator rolled into one. Failure becomes an arrow pointing you in the right direction.

When faced with a failure, here are a few suggestions about what to do next: Set a timer for 15 minutes and allow yourself a little wallow; call your best friend; tape the failure to your refrigerator as a reminder of what it feels like to try and to care. When you're ready, share your attempts with other people. You can encourage them to go after their own goals, and they can cheer you on when you start again.

But here's what not to do: Never allow yourself to feel that trying was a waste of time, or that one minor setback is a final judgment on your talent, skills, or ability. Putting yourself out there for an opportunity—whether it's a job, competition, grant, or anything else—is a brave and hopeful risk.

You want it.

You want something.

Let this truth clarify and motivate all your moves.

So what should you do with this fresh new knowledge?

Hear me out for a second: I think you should write a thank-you note to your failure.

Why not send a genuine, nonsarcastic message to whoever (or whatever) turned you down? And no, this isn't a passive-aggressive trick to make someone else feel bad. What's past has passed. Writing a thank-you note helps refocus; this one moment won't define your life, your year, or even your day. Sending the note is a promise to yourself that you will survive.

If you're comfortable with the idea, write one in these pages. Search for words that feel accurate and authentic. To help you begin, here are notes I've sent over the years after various failures and rejections.

> *I wanted to thank you for your timely response (you said "early March" and that it is!) and for creating this lab. Support for screenwriters often arrives in abstract or expensive ways, and I'm grateful to the festival for providing a substantive way for writers to grow and develop their work. I look forward to submitting in the future.*

> *Thank you for considering my work for this year's program. This opportunity allowed me to refine and develop my pilot, and I'm excited about what comes next. We all need some encouragement this year, and knowing there were keen eyes on the other end of this submission gave me that extra push to polish this draft.*

Sending these notes gave me a sense of closure and allowed me to separate the "accepted or rejected" binary from my creativity. They refocused my energy, reminded me creating and submitting can be thrilling, and helped me imagine what lies ahead. And they opened my eyes to the fact that there are actual people on the other end of every opportunity—real people who took time and energy to evaluate my work. Who knows, I may even encounter them again one day.

I've never regretted reframing a rejection into a positive interaction, but I've definitely regretted spending months (or years) agonizing over plans that never came to fruition. There is a deep peace that comes from giving thanks and moving on. Because what you also wanted—and what you received—was the chance to show up and be seen.

Remember that one moment does not define every moment. One failure does not mean *you* are a failure. Failure can create an essential map leading you toward your future. Look back and you'll probably find a few examples. Maybe while you were waiting for an update after a job interview, you decided to pivot and apply to graduate school. Or the company you were so eager to join ended up dissolving shortly after you would have started. Or your future boss, the one who convinced you to apply, accepted another job and moved to Japan.

Anything can happen, and you never know what will happen, so give thanks for the invisible favors you cannot see. Trust that this specific opportunity wasn't for you for a very good reason.

You have taken a risk. You remain hopeful. You are grateful and you have grown. You will learn and move on.

Try, celebrate your failures, give thanks, repeat.

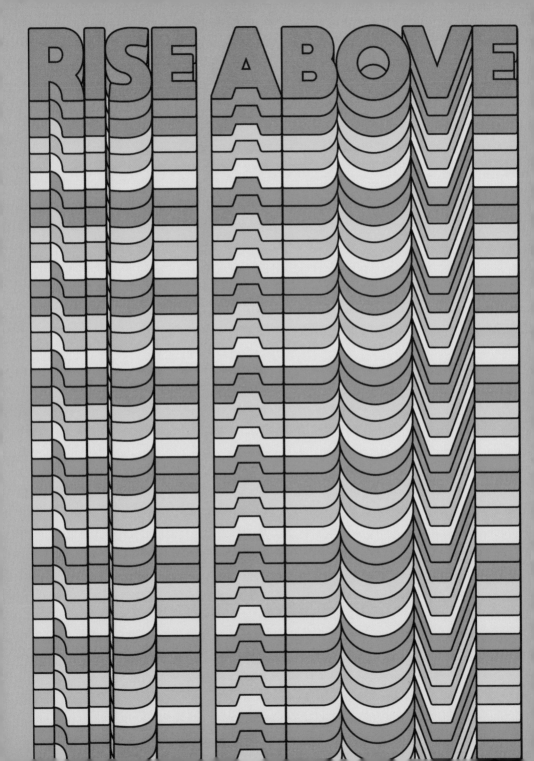

What is one failure you've experienced lately?

Draft a thank-you note to that failure right here.

Dear _____

_____

_____

_____

_____

_____

_____

_____

_____

_____

_____

_____

_____

_____

_____

Think about a friend who is facing failure at the moment.

What advice would you give them?

Can you apply these words to your own situation?

Time to rack up some tiny failures!

List five times you tried and came up short this week.

What did you learn from each situation?

1. _____

_____

2. _____

_____

3. _____

_____

4. _____

_____

5. _____

_____

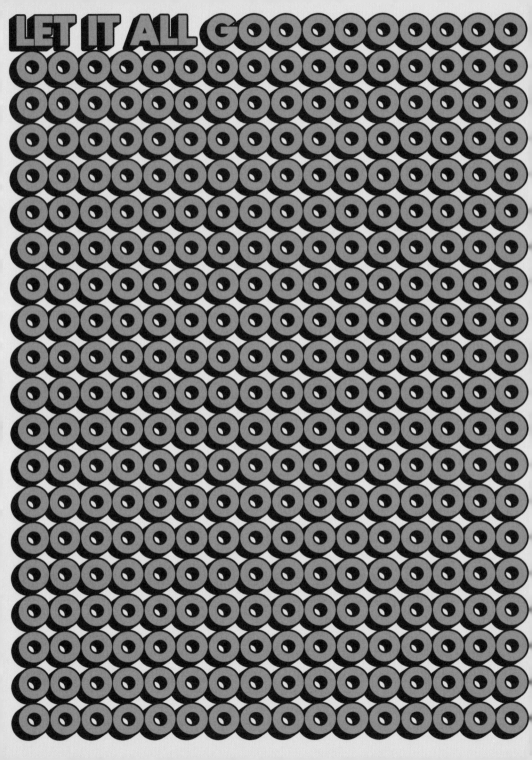

What have you
failed to begin?

What does bouncing back feel like?

_____

_____

_____

_____

_____

_____

_____

_____

_____

_____

_____

_____

_____

_____

EVERYONE IS JUST TRYING THEIR BEST WITH THE INFORMATION THEY HAVE

Rejection spins us in new directions.

Consider a circumstance that seemed like a failure, but that now looks like a good thing. **What happened—and why are you grateful it didn't work out?**

Pretend you're throwing a party for your failure.

Go as over-the-top as you'd like—this is your last chance to say good-bye before you move on.

Where would it be? What would you do? Who would you invite? Design the invitation here.

CHAPTER 06

Weave a Generous Web

Everyone wants the perfect mentor, someone who can help you clarify the next moves in your life and career, thanks to having a kind heart or being a trusted confidante.

The idea sounds great on paper, and finding a mentor is a worthwhile pursuit, yet it is also a time-consuming one. Mentors might be busy with their own projects. (They're successful, that's why you admire them.) But you don't have to wait for a mentor to give you all the answers. Instead, if you want to move forward, you should search for two different types of people: champions and collaborators.

A champion is someone who supports you—full stop. This could be a family member, colleague, boss, even a Twitter acquaintance. You probably already have a few champions in your life. They take you seriously and cheer you on. They show up. They say yes. They engage. They brainstorm. They have deep conversations.

One champion might provide life advice, another could be great at asking illuminating questions, and a third may be a savant of career strategies. One champion shouldn't be expected to do *everything*, but they can provide honesty, guidance, or simply enthusiasm. Ideally, you have woven a wide web of champions with different skills who are glad to hang out in your corner (and you're glad to hang

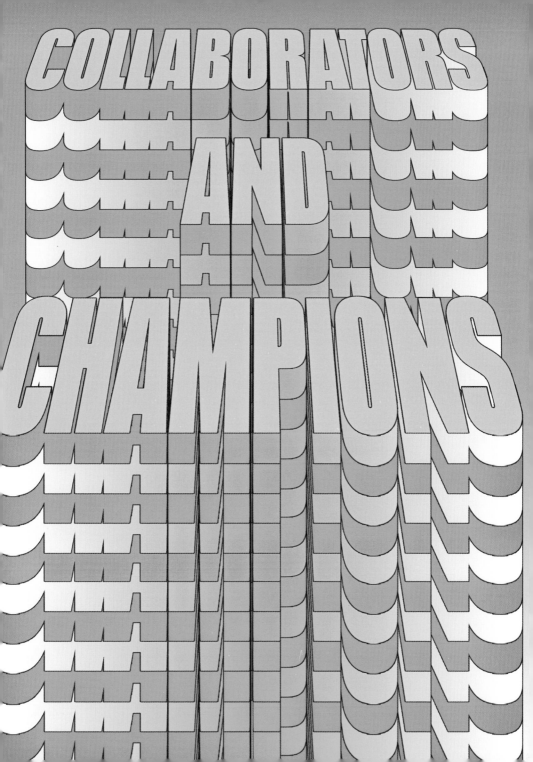

out in theirs). By the way, this isn't networking—at least not in the traditional way. Instead, you're simply making connections with people you like.

Collaborators are the other building blocks of a life in forward motion. Let's use this term loosely. Anyone you're working with on a project can (and should) be a collaborator. A baseball team scatters onto the field, takes their positions, and trusts that each player will do their job and give their best effort. You should have that same level of trust with your collaborators. Have confidence that they will do their jobs, and hopefully they will extend that confidence to you.

Where do you find champions and collaborators? The short answer: Look for people who uplift others.

You know it when you see it. A few years ago, a humor writer kept coming up in my Twitter feed, even though I didn't follow her. But I saw her name because she made encouraging comments about other people's work, suggested insightful articles to read, and congratulated friends when they posted good news. I thought, *Caitlin seems so positive! She is someone I'd like to know.* (We're now friends, and it's no surprise that she's the definition of a champion.)

Some champions are already in your life; others you might have to seek out. Every job, project, or picnic for a friend of a friend gives you a chance to meet someone who can change your path. You might change theirs, too—this isn't a one-way relationship, and this is not about creating an army of supporters. The best and most effective way to find champions and collaborators is to be an excellent one yourself.

When you meet someone new, ask about what excites them. Follow their enthusiasm. Support their work. Read, like, boost, and share. Connect with others, and you'll find that energy comes back to you tenfold.

And as you're weaving this web of generous people, it's important to keep in mind there is so much happening that we don't see.

The editor ghosting you and your draft might be dealing with a health crisis. The friend who never responded to your text may be watching their relationship crumble. Your moody boss could be at their own career crossroads. There could be less-consequential reasons why someone is out of touch or drifting away.

You rarely know the full story. And yet it's easy to make judgments, rail against issues out of our control, or spin narratives about people without acknowledging that every person is the main character in their own lives, and they are each dealing with unseen issues, conflicts, and crises, too. Living in this world is a full-time job. We can try to be decent, kind, and understanding. And we can try to be generous in our assumptions about others.

My friend Selina and I like to call this kind of generosity *being magnanimous*. (We actually call it *being magnanimous AF*, but you don't need the acronym for it to work.) You don't have to dedicate yourself to complete selflessness or lapse into martyrdom—there is such a thing as going overboard!—but it's more about being generous with your time, energy, and expectations.

So what does this look like in practice?

It means not making wild assumptions about someone else's silence. Avoiding statements or actions that feel inauthentic. Listening to your gut reactions. Being genuinely interested in how someone is doing, what they're working on, and ways you might be able to help, to an extent that feels true to you.

Being magnanimous means sharing your time, knowledge, or presence. It's not about blindly believing another person's intentions are always good—sometimes they're not—but instead operating with the knowledge that *your* intentions can primarily be good.

Lead with generosity and people will want to know you and work with you. Why not extend the web of generosity to the folks already in your life, to strangers you encounter for a short time, and—perhaps most importantly—to yourself?

Cheering on people who are succeeding, trying, or taking a risk always feels better than the sting of envy. Show enthusiasm for the work you share, the friends you meet, and the projects you begin or are brave enough to see through.

Instead of wondering how someone can help you, consider how you can become a great champion for them. One of my favorite sayings about the power of collaboration is: "A rising tide lifts all boats." Sometimes we're the tide, other times we're the boat.

Either way, we have the choice to be a part of something greater than ourselves.

Think of a friend,
family member,
or colleague who
makes you feel
confident in your
ideas.

Imagine they are cheering
you on and want to hear
about what you're working on.

**What would you be excited
to share with them?**

Write a thank-you note to one of your biggest champions.

Dear _____

_____

_____

_____

_____

_____

_____

_____

_____

_____

_____

_____

_____

_____

What is one way
you can nurture an
existing relationship
or friendship today?

_____

_____

_____

_____

_____

_____

_____

_____

_____

_____

_____

_____

_____

_____

Who would be a dream collaborator?

What would they bring to your project?

_____

_____

_____

_____

_____

_____

_____

_____

_____

_____

_____

_____

_____

_____

_____

Has someone you know received good news lately?

Tell them right here how you feel about their accomplishment—and then tell them in person, if you'd like.

_____

_____

_____

_____

_____

_____

_____

_____

_____

_____

_____

_____

_____

_____

_____

_____

_____

DREAMS START ON THE GROUND

CHAPTER 07

Share Your Wealth

My favorite person in the world was my Grandpa Cotti. He lived to the age of ninety-nine, and his mind was sharp until the very end. His favorite pastime was bingo, but if you're picturing a leisurely game with a slow-drawling bingo caller, think again: He played at a local casino, and these games were *intense*.

But what I remember most about bingo was my grandpa's habit of slipping a few dollars to the people who helped him, from the kind woman who brought him coffee to the golf cart driver who picked him up curbside. They adored him. I once asked my grandpa if tipping was always a practice for him, and he said, with his characteristic grin, "Share your wealth . . . what little there is."

Wealth doesn't have to mean money: sometimes it comes in the form of time, energy, or a work in progress that you want to share with someone else, or that someone wants to share with you.

Sharing is hard. It's easier to keep our thoughts or drafts hidden away, because if no one sees them, no one critiques them. And yet, I'm convinced that sharing is a kind of wonder drug, if you're brave enough to do it. Remembering how scary it is to share something can also help you support people who are brave enough to share with you. Making one kind comment takes little effort, but the other person might remember it for months.

LOOK AT ALL THAT YOU HAVE

There's an energy to sharing; it makes you believe you can take on the world. (Because you can.) Every story, or piece of art, or secret dream you share—even if it's with just one other person—is a brave act. It can give you confidence to stare down gatekeepers and critics and say, "Bring it on." Sharing means climbing the wall, peering over the other side into the dark water, not knowing how deep or cold it might be—and descending into the unknown.

"Share early and often" can be your motto, too. The more you do it, the less afraid you'll be to do it again.

Share your good news. Your mistakes and failures. Your idealism and aspirations. Share your works in progress. Your vulnerabilities. Your favorite things, the ones that matter most to you. Share your experience, expertise, and advice. Share your desire for help. Share your counsel and connections. Your boundaries. The soundtrack underscoring your life. Share your hopes for the future.

All of this sharing lightens the burdens of living. You feel buoyant because your work now exists outside of you. A bonus: Your work gets sharper and clearer because you have to explain it to someone else.

Sharing can put you in the spotlight—that might make you nervous, but have faith that you belong. The spotlight is where you grow, learn, revise, and create yourself.

Of course, there is some risk involved, especially if your goal or dream is in its early stages. But when you declare, "Look, I made this," you're proving to yourself that you're brave, moving forward, and unafraid.

Maybe—OK—you're a *tiny bit* afraid.

What if everyone laughs? They might think your painting is hideous, your short story is half-baked, or your business idea is five years behind the curve. Everyone might say, "Who is *she* to be giving advice?" or "Shouldn't you stick to your original plan?" Everyone's probably sitting in a big room giggling about your mistakes or burning up a group chat, dissecting your every move.

But let me ask you: Who is *everyone*?

Everyone does not include your champions or collaborators. *Everyone* is not your ideal readers or audience (assuming *everyone*, in fact, exists, and there's a high probability they don't). Let their whispers be carried away in the wind.

Trust that your work will find the people who need it. This isn't to say that every experience is going to be perfect or rewarding. Sometimes you will share your work and then want to crawl into the deepest hole you can find. I know the feeling.

In the first year of my musical theater workshop, we were told to write a comedy song. A gifted composer and I wrote a fun number for a character from a Wendy Wasserstein play. (The workshop prides itself on difficult assignments.) We had a rehearsal, and I thought, *Wow, this song sounds great!* The moment came to perform in front of the class. Our talented singer took his place and sang his heart out, hitting every joke. And no one laughed. The problem was straightforward enough: The song wasn't funny.

The composer and I had to stand there and hear feedback about exactly why it didn't work. My cheeks were burning. I avoided looking at my friends. I wondered why I ever believed I'd be able to write songs. (At that moment I thought, *Some people have talent, some people don't*.) When our session was over, I slid into the back row of class and wanted to disappear.

And then something amazing happened . . .

Absolutely nothing.

No one told me I didn't belong. I wasn't escorted out of the building. And I realized I had experienced my worst-case scenario. I bombed—but I lived. Even better, I learned what not to do the next time. (For the record, don't choose an unfunny scene to musicalize, and stick to a clear rhyme scheme.)

This is an example of why we must keep sharing, even in the face of possible failure or embarrassment. Offering up a small part of ourselves reminds us of the messiness and possibilities of being alive. We see what works, and what might need a little more work.

How many ideas, projects, and dreams have you kept inside? How often do you say, "I'll get to that soon," or "No one will understand this"? Neat excuses for staying still. It's much easier to blame an outside critic than to blame yourself.

But the truth about sharing is that no one will ever love your work as much as you want them to anyway. They can't. They are engaged in their own lives, and their approval is not your engine—and you don't need it to be.

It's important to get clear on your expectations before sharing something. I like to ask myself, "What do I honestly *want* to hear?"

Usually, the answer is one of the following:

- Praise or encouragement to keep going (especially true for projects in the early stages of development)
- General, overarching feedback about whether this is a viable idea
- Detailed and truthful notes
- Raw and unfiltered comments

Here's the kicker: *You can guide the feedback of the other person*. If you send a story draft to a friend, you can tell them, "I just started this piece, so I'm looking for comments on whether this is working and you were engaged," or, if you want to get more specific, "I'm submitting this to a journal next week. Can you please copy edit every line?"

Above all, be clear with what you're asking and protect your project. I once casually mentioned a screenplay I was working on to a coworker and she said, "Wasn't there already a movie like that a few years back? Those kind of films are so hard to do right." Her response sent me reeling. But I wasn't looking for feedback from her in that moment, even though that's what I received. Truthfully, I probably shouldn't have mentioned it at all. The idea was in its early stages, and she wasn't one of my champions or collaborators. When you're ready to share widely, take in comments or advice that feel useful to you and feel free to discard the rest. The value lies in you being brave enough to share, not in your ability to change your idea based on other people's comments.

Because we do not sustain ourselves with likes, hearts, or applause. We survive by sharing what only *we* can share and knowing that, at least in this one brief moment, we had a little bit of courage.

Perhaps when you share you will encounter a *Yes* or a *Keep going*. Or you might find . . . nothing. But even in the face of silence or a shrug, you will be okay. You will survive.

You already heard one *yes*.

It was the yes you said to yourself.

Consider two places where you can share your work.

What would you like to hear from each arena that would help move your project forward?

SHARE YOUR TRUTH

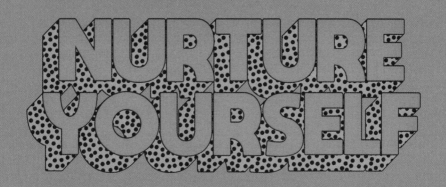

NURTURE YOURSELF

SO YOU CAN

NURTURE OTHERS

Name three people
in your life who
provide safe spaces
to share your works
in progress.

1.
_____

2.
_____

3.
_____

Think back to a time when you shared something and felt embarrassed by the outcome.

What happened immediately afterward? How do you feel about it now?

What did you learn from the experience?

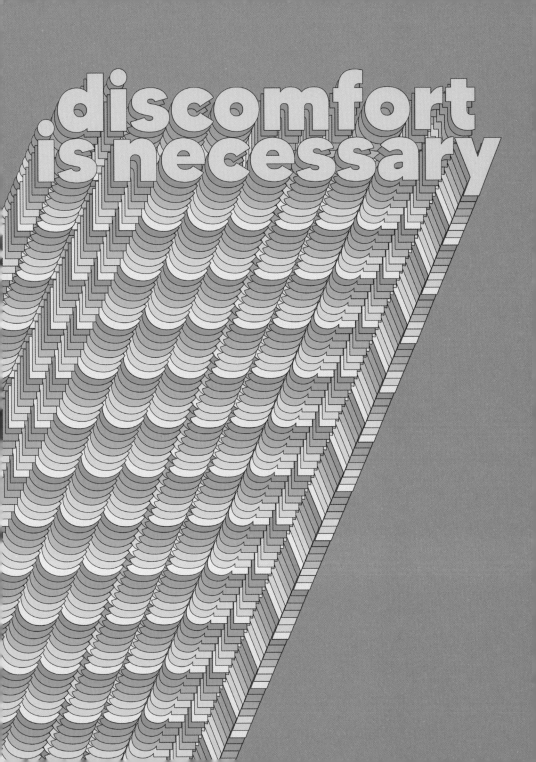

IT IS ONLY AS

MEANINGFUL

AS YOU DECIDE

IT SHOULD BE

Who are you afraid is going to judge your work?

Why might that fear be realistic or not?

Declare a big intention here.

I am a _____ and I am working toward

_____.

My ultimate goal is _____

_____.

How did that feel? When
might you feel comfortable
sharing that intention with
someone else?

What is one piece
of advice someone
shared with you
lately?

How did it change you?

What can you create today and share with one person?

CHAPTER 08

Do It Today

We've all been there.

You know when you have a project to work on, but you just can't get moving?

That was my problem not long ago. I was supposed to finish writing the journal you're reading right now.

Telling myself I had a deadline didn't work. Imagining the readers or the audience it could reach didn't help either (and created unnecessary pressure). Bribing myself only led to more procrastination.

But the irony was I wanted to do the work. I was excited about it. Laziness, poor planning, or lack of time weren't what stopped me. It was fear. Fear that it wouldn't live up to the vision in my head, that I would fail, that it would be a waste of time. That fear of creating something imperfect stopped me from finishing.

Why do we want so badly for everything to be perfect right away? What is the rush? Beginners want to be experts and experts want their work to feel exciting and new. No one is immune to feelings of inadequacy or stagnation or impostor syndrome. If it weren't so frustrating, it would almost be kind of beautiful, the immense amount of wanting that surrounds us.

The obvious advice is: Be happy with what you have—you don't need to try so hard.

DO,

DON'T OVERDO

But it's possible to be happy and still want more. You can continue to search for moments and projects and people that give meaning to your days. You can find satisfaction in striving. You can take big swings and set audacious goals while absorbing the lessons taught by rejection and failure.

But it all comes down to one little action: doing.

Do something. Consider your options. Change your mind. Share. Debate. Percolate. Move. Commit. Do something. You are a verb, remember. You're not a noun.

You must do the thing eating away the heart of you. There is no other choice.

And, if you haven't noticed already, you have been doing something, right here and now. You were brave enough to begin, brave enough to come all this way. Now you must be brave enough to continue.

As you move ahead, keep in mind something I've learned over and over again: There is no finish line.

That might sound daunting. But after starting, pushing through (or yes, even abandoning) many projects, I've seen the mirage of the finish line. I'd tell myself, *If only I could hear that song performed,* or *If only I was accepted into that fellowship,* then I would enter some magical promised land of competence, mastery, or approval that would "fix" my career and life.

Sometimes we do reach new heights or grab these achievements, and they feel like wonderful accomplishments. But soon, our eyes will begin darting around again, looking for another beginning. This is the nature of living. As major milestones distance and die, you will want new challenges. You will begin again. You will follow the pull.

Accepting there is no single, concrete finish line can help you sustain momentum. You don't have one target. You have forever—and that is a gift.

Trust that you have plenty of time to create, adjust, learn, and continue trying. Yes, there might be dry spells or stumbles along the way. You might find yourself spinning or searching for a linear path.

But linear paths are boring. They are not for you. To move forward, return to the commitment you made to yourself: Do it. Do it today. Do it now.

Try to remember, this is not about hustling harder or putting unrealistic demands on yourself. Do, don't overdo.

More will happen than you can imagine. Committing to action leads you to doing something more often than not. Doing means you're changing, developing, investing, sacrificing, and growing. You will feel the flash of forward motion, the spark of momentum, and the joy that arrives with doing meaningful work. And meaningful work can lead to a more meaningful life.

A meaningful life looks like a house that's being endlessly renovated, but in the best possible way—your contractor is efficient, your interior decorator has excellent taste, and they're both you. There is no final brick to lay, no perfect paint color to choose. Your budget is unlimited, and you get to keep adding on rooms and floors. Want a sixth bedroom? Great! Feel like ripping out the new carpet? Why not! You'll rearrange the furniture hundreds of times and fall in love and be surprised with your space over and over again.

As you're building and creating, look around. Your old house—your old life—will be unrecognizable.

This renovation is an offering—you don't have to do one thing forever. Some projects will eventually move from your brain and heart to the page or the public. Others will not. Some jobs will expand and set you toward a new destination. Others might disappear. Some friendships and relationships will bloom as the years pass. Others might fade.

But through it all, you can return to the practice of doing.

Always remember: ·

Follow your curiosity.

Start before you're ready.

Percolate your ideas.

Find courage to fly.

Show off your rejections with pride.

Connect with your champions.

Share your generous spirit.

Cultivate optimism.

Keep going. Keep moving. You have a choice.

Do it today—and you'll do it for life.

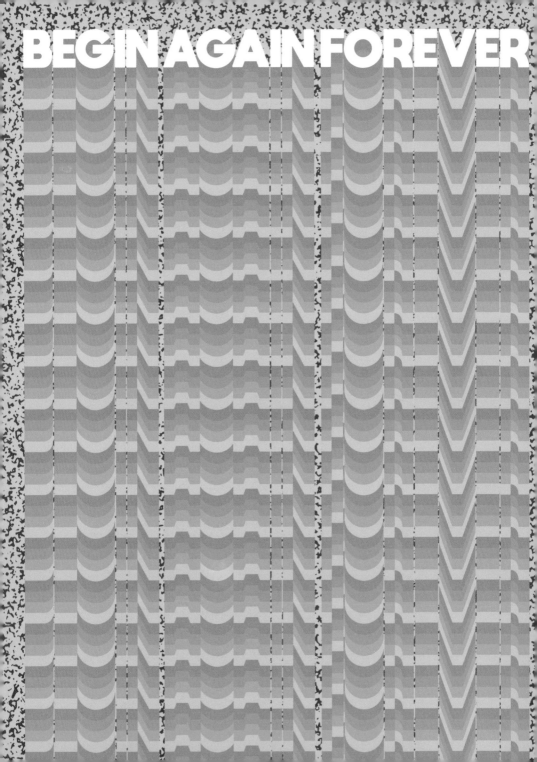

What are you
excited to begin?

Describe a time when you felt like you were *overdoing* it.

What did you take away from that experience?

Name one action
or decision that
you've put off
doing or making.

Why haven't you moved
forward on this yet?

**How can you help yourself
today?**

What are you feeling pulled to finish?

Write about the finish line for something that's on your mind.

What does it look like? How real does it seem to you?

_____

_____

_____

_____

_____

_____

_____

_____

_____

_____

_____

_____

_____

_____

_____

Create. Adjust.
Learn. Try.

**How do these words apply
to your life right now?**

_____

_____

_____

_____

_____

_____

_____

_____

_____

_____

_____

_____

_____

_____

What can you commit to doing today?

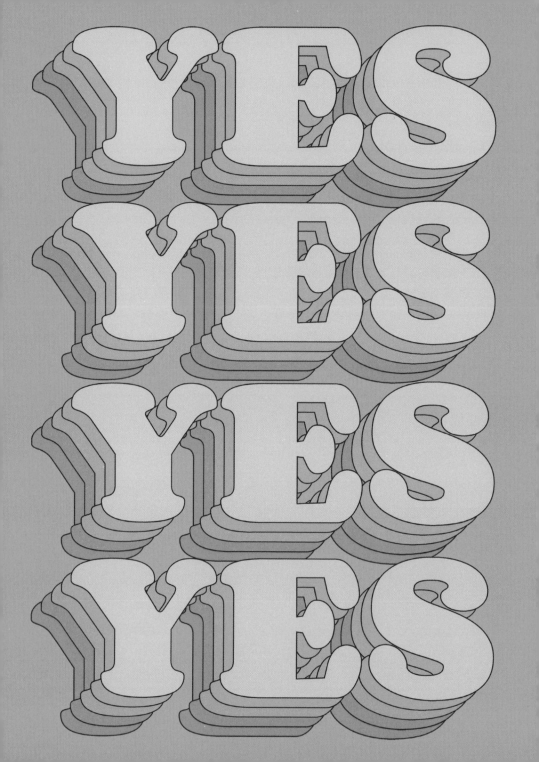

You've made it.

**What does a meaningful life
look like to you at this moment?**

Editor: Zack Knoll
Designer: Diane Shaw
Managing Editor: Glenn Ramirez
Production Manager: Kathleen Gaffney

ISBN: 978-1-4197-6402-8

ABRAMS The Art of Books
195 Broadway, New York, NY 10007
abramsbooks.com